Introduction 1

Caterpillar® is the world's leading manufacturer of construction and mining equipment, diesel and natural gas engines, industrial gas turbines and diesel-electric locomotives. We are a leader and proudly have the largest global presence in the industries we serve.

The history of Caterpillar® is all about doing: creating, building, problem solving, innovating, testing, servicing and improving. Enjoy the ingenious machines from our rich heritage, and more importantly, the people who founded and built the company one breakthrough at a time. Beginning with Benjamin Holt and C. L. Best, the people of Caterpillar® have always been – and continue to be – extraordinary.

We want you to learn about our company and our equipment. Meet these fun characters and help them complete this activity and coloring book.

CHOMPER the Compactor

A compactor is a machine or mechanism used to reduce the size of material such as waste material or bio mass through compaction. A trash compactor is often used by a home or business to reduce the volume of trash it produces. ... Normally powered by hydraulics, compactors take many shapes and sizes.

DALE the Dozer

A bulldozer is a powerful tractor with a broad upright blade at the front for clearing ground.

2 Introduction

ELLIE the Excavator

An excavator is a large machine for removing soil from the ground, especially on a building site.

SCOOTER the Skid-Steer Loader

A skid loader, skid-steer loader or skidsteer is a small, rigid-frame, engine-powered machine with lift arms used to attach a wide variety of labor-saving tools or attachments.

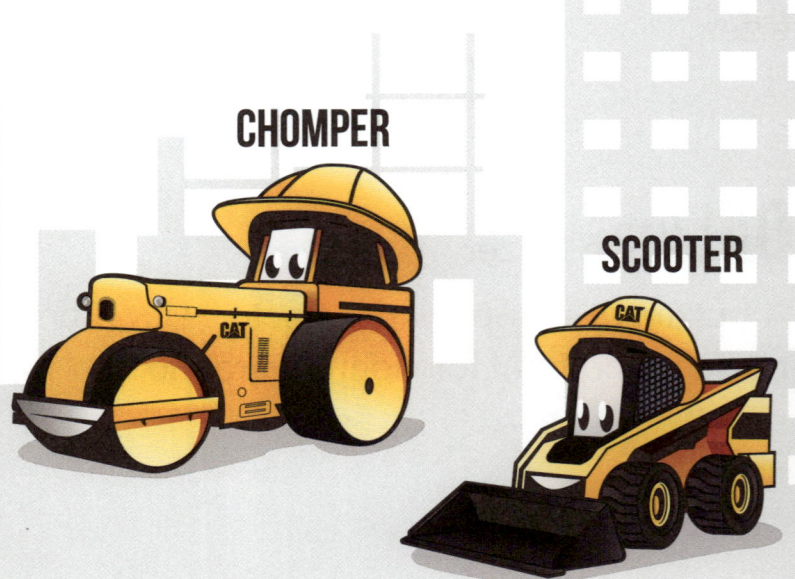

ELLIE

DALE

CHOMPER

SCOOTER

Coloring 3

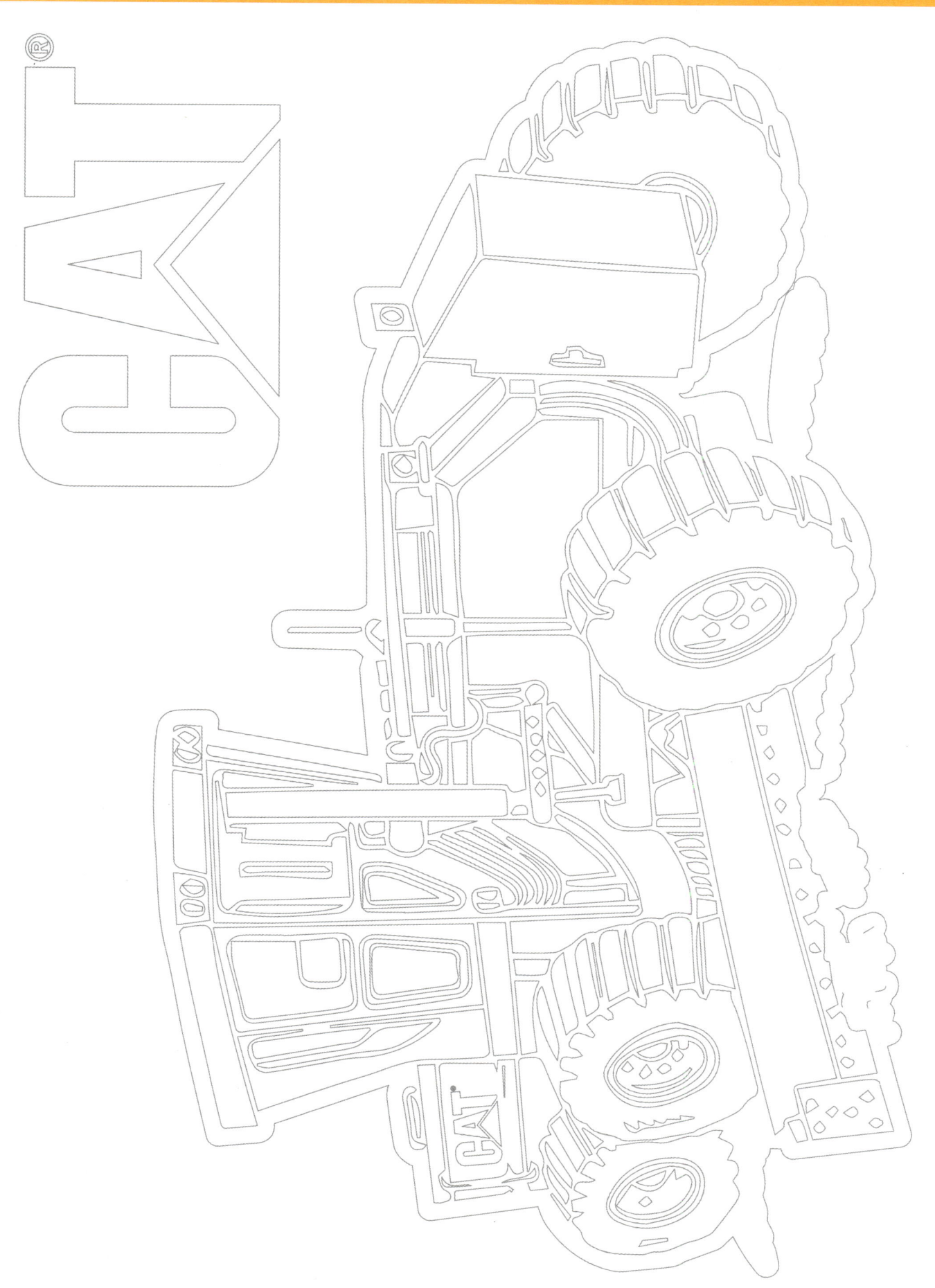

4 Drawing

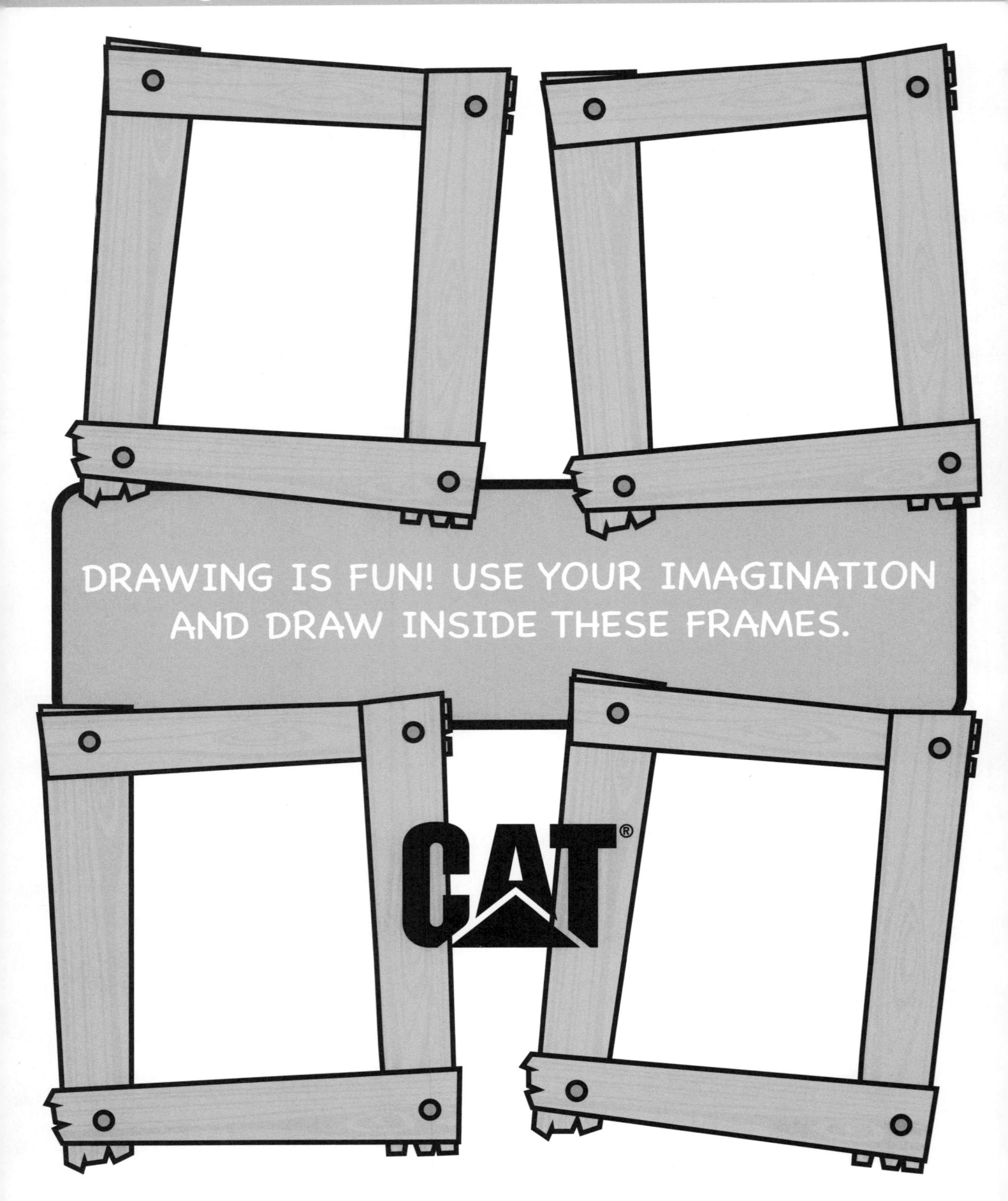

DRAWING IS FUN! USE YOUR IMAGINATION AND DRAW INSIDE THESE FRAMES.

HELP CHOMPER GET TO WORK!

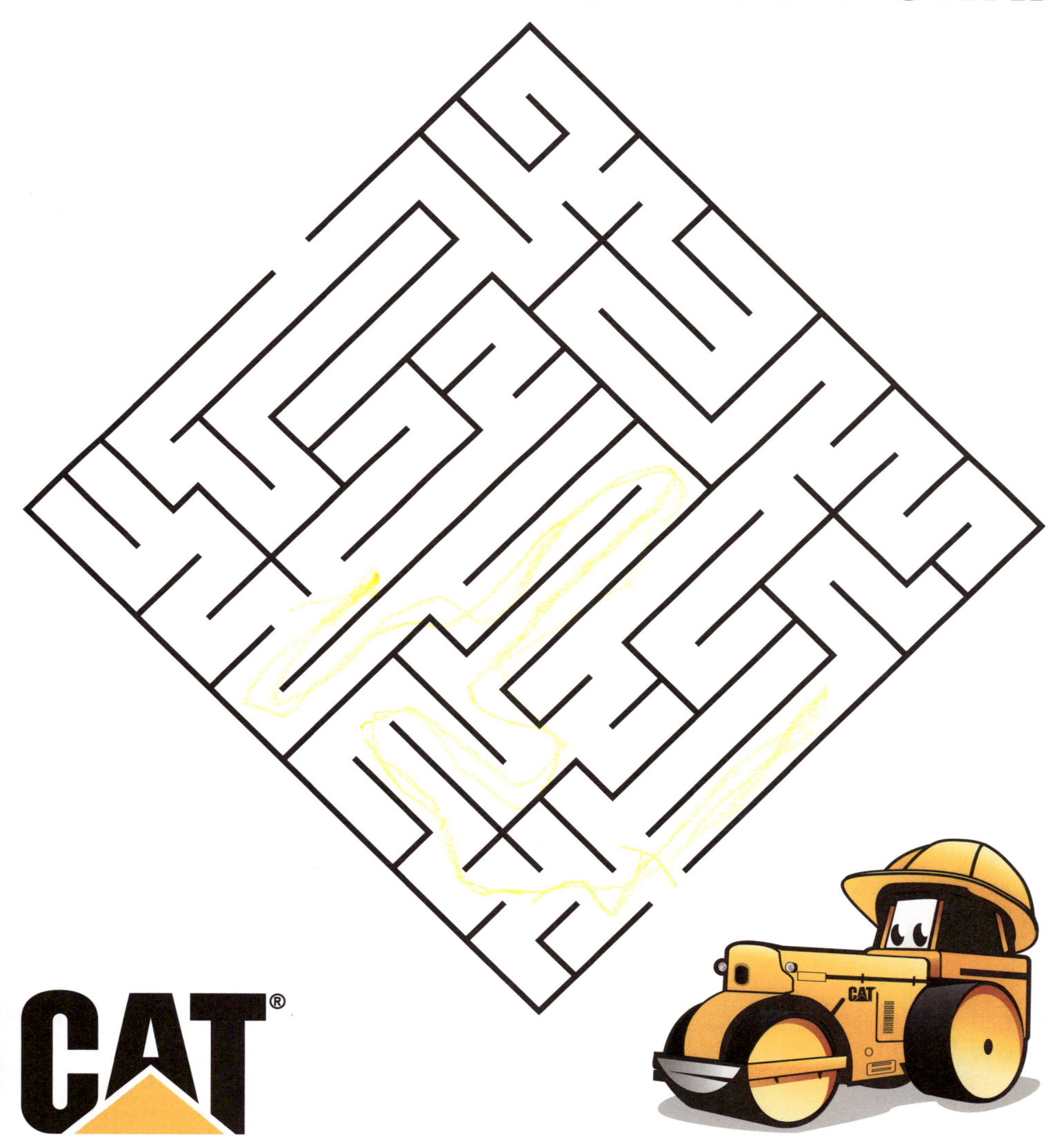

Maze 5

CAT

6 Drawing

What is today's project?
Draw it in the space below.

CAT®

Coloring 7

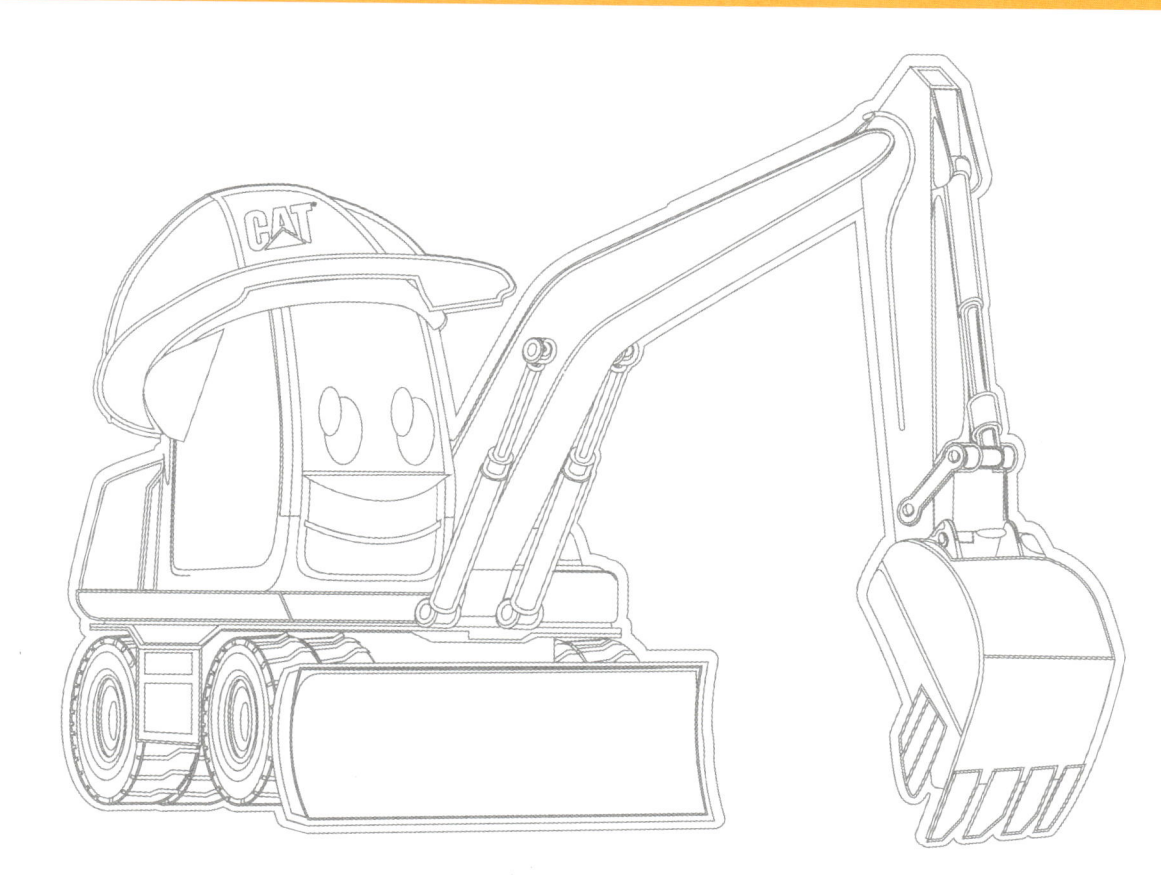

DESIGN & COLOR YOUR OWN.

8 Drawing

Draw your dream house.
What color would it be? How many bedrooms would it have?
What would your yard look like?
Be creative!

CAT®

Connect the Dots

Connect the Dots 9

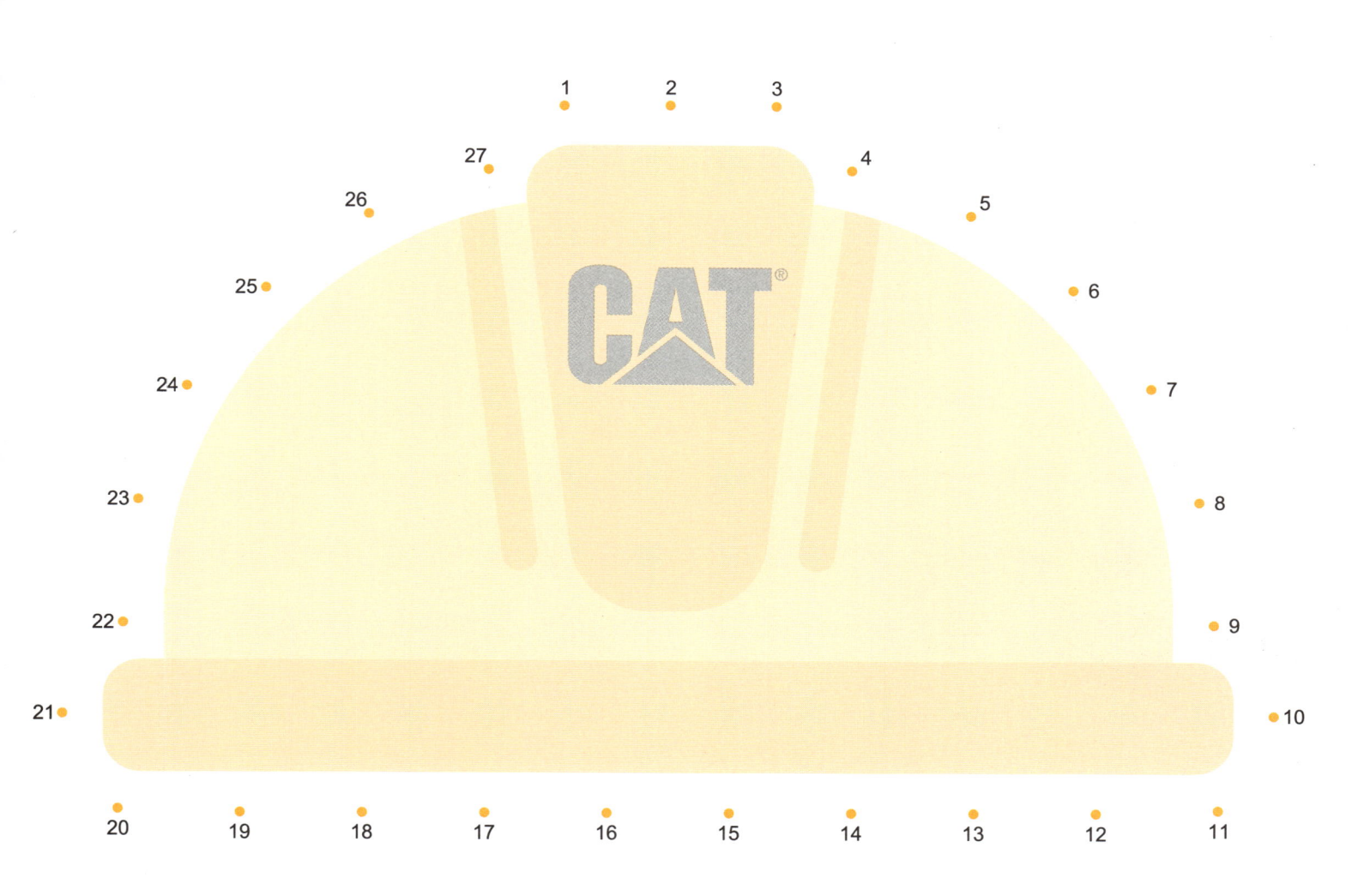

CAT

10 Word Search

```
P H A C O T R E E X D S S M P
F Z T I A M N E V U R M Y L K
D L T R T T Y E R I B T S F Y
V Z A V E O E A M T R T T J T
J V C I L L B R X P E D E Y I
V T H P V L I Y P C I X M L N
J T M D E Y K A H I J U S Q U
K E E V U H V N B E L P Q T M
R C N A C D O M O L L K E M
O Z T G D L H R P E E D A J O
W Y S E O M A C H I N E S R C
O L X G S V A F G B Z Q Z A Z
J Z Y P I H S R E D A E L G T
S T R A P X L R F C M R I Y U
W P N M U F S W X C G D X E F
```

CAN YOU FIND THESE WORDS?

ATTACHMENTS • CATERPILLAR • COMMUNITY • DIG
DRIVE • DURABLE • EMPLOYEE • EQUIPMENT
LEADERSHIP • MACHINES • PARTS • RELIABLE
SYSTEMS • TECHNOLOGY • WORK

Draw Your Own Cat® Machine 11

Draw the machine and name what it does.

12 Draw Your Own Cat® Machine

Coloring 13

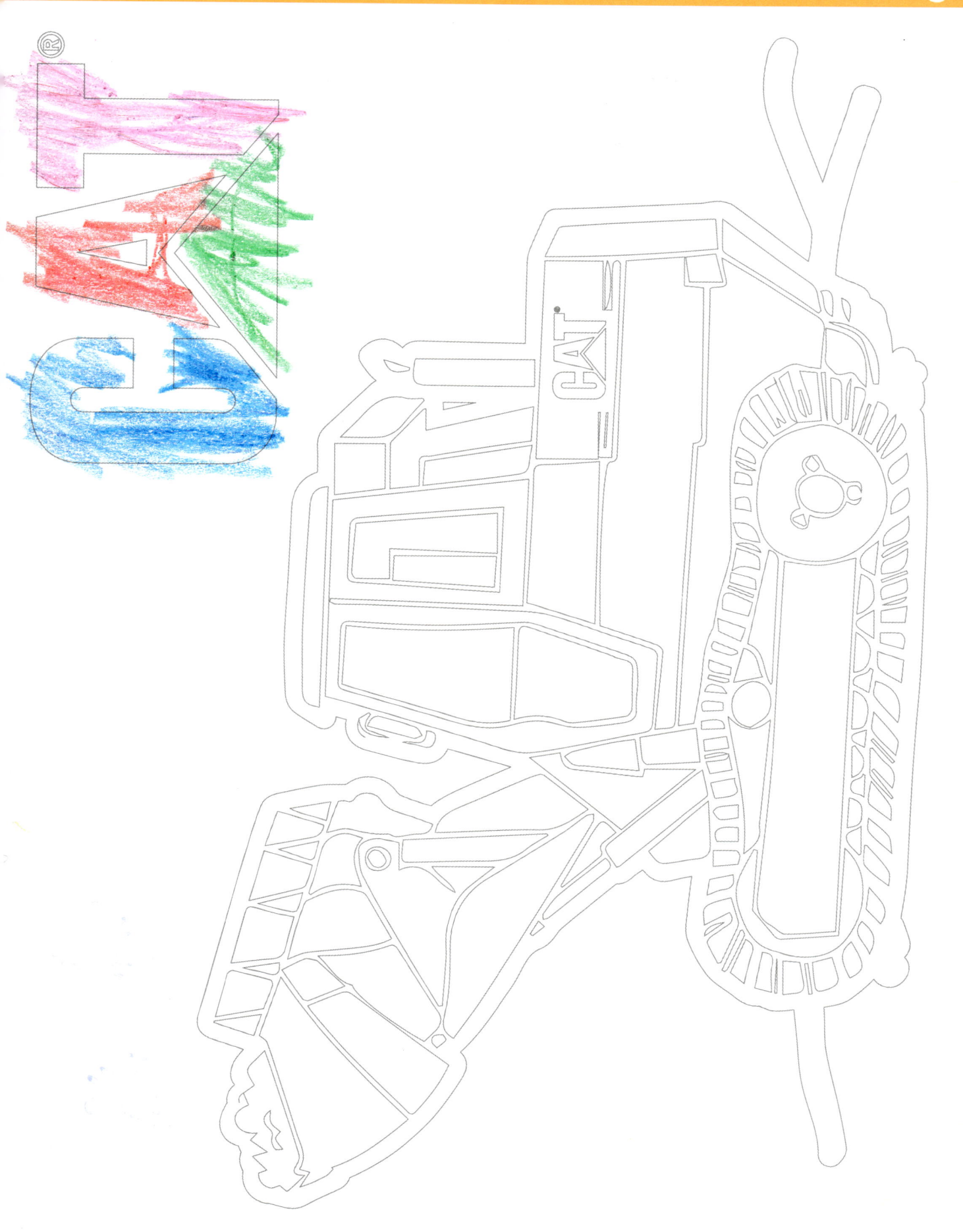

14 Drawing

WHAT DO YOU WANT TO BE WHEN YOU GROW UP?

WHEN YOU GET OLDER, YOU COULD WORK FOR CAT®! LOOK IN THE MIRRORS AND DRAW YOURSELF!

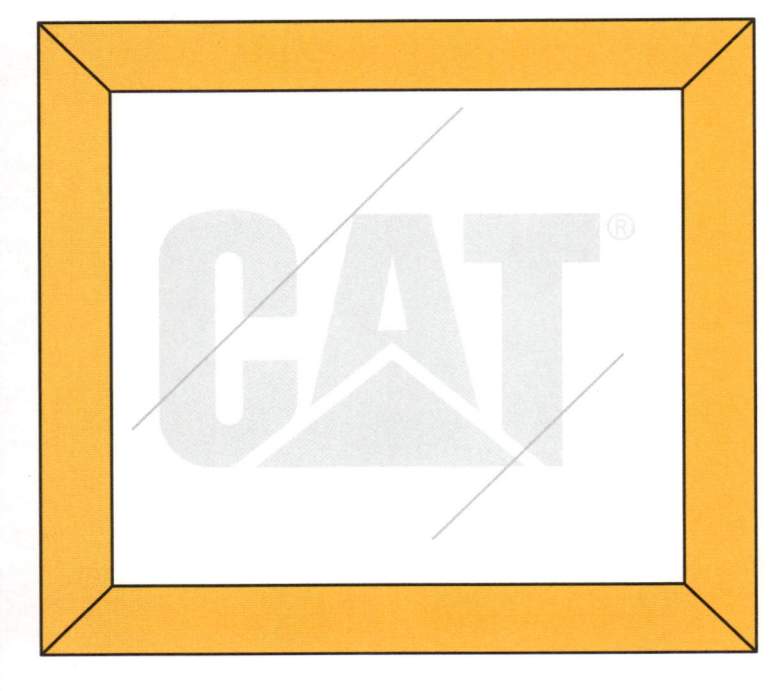

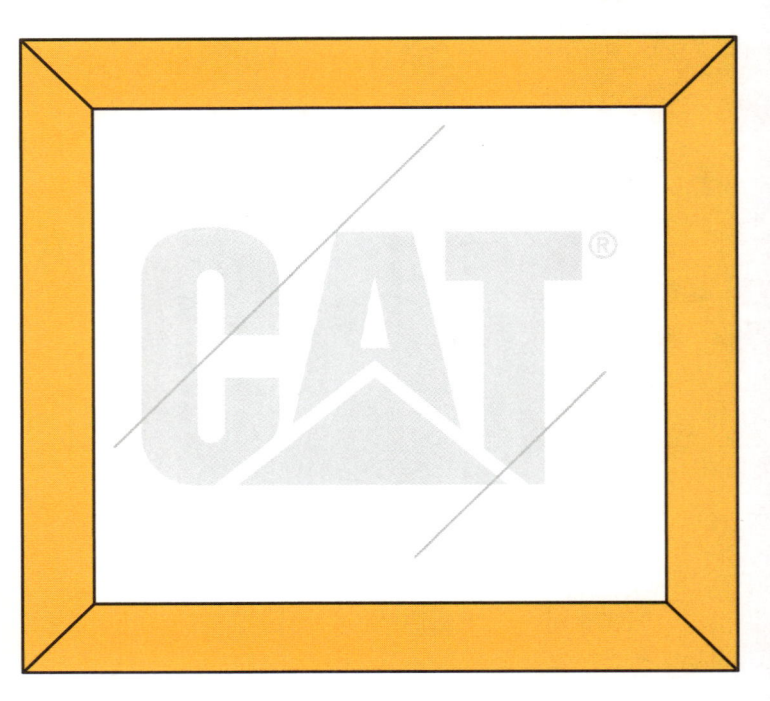

Maze 15

HELP ELLIE GET TO THE PILES OF SOIL

16 Cat® Challenge

DRAW A LINE FROM THE ARROW ➡ TO THE STAR ★, CONNECTING ONLY LOADERS TO COMPACTORS OR COMPACTORS TO LOADERS

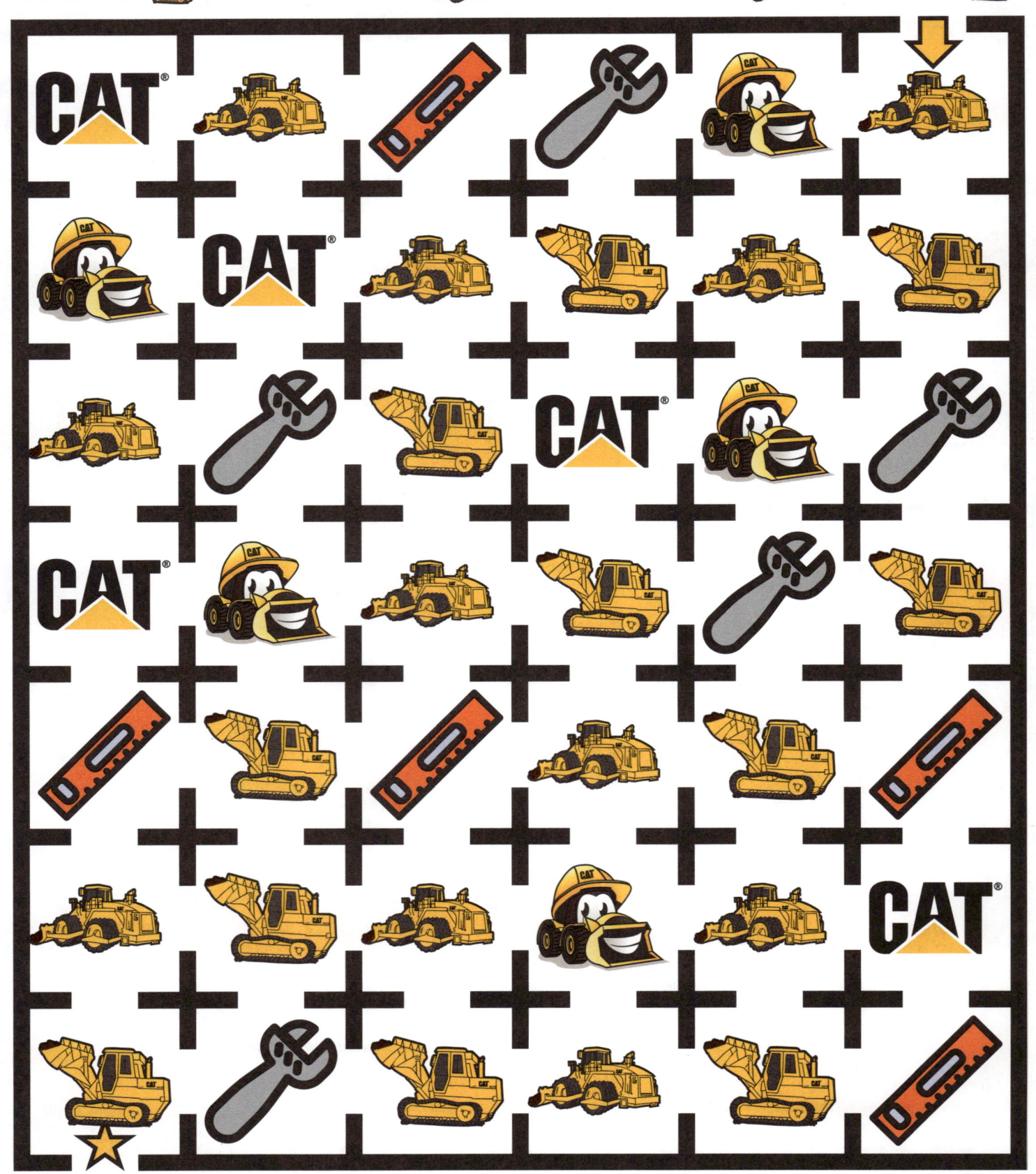

Drawing 17

CREATE YOUR OWN CAT® BOOKMARK

18 Drawing

CREATE YOUR OWN CAT® BOOKMARK

Games 19

TIC-TAC-TOE

20 Maze

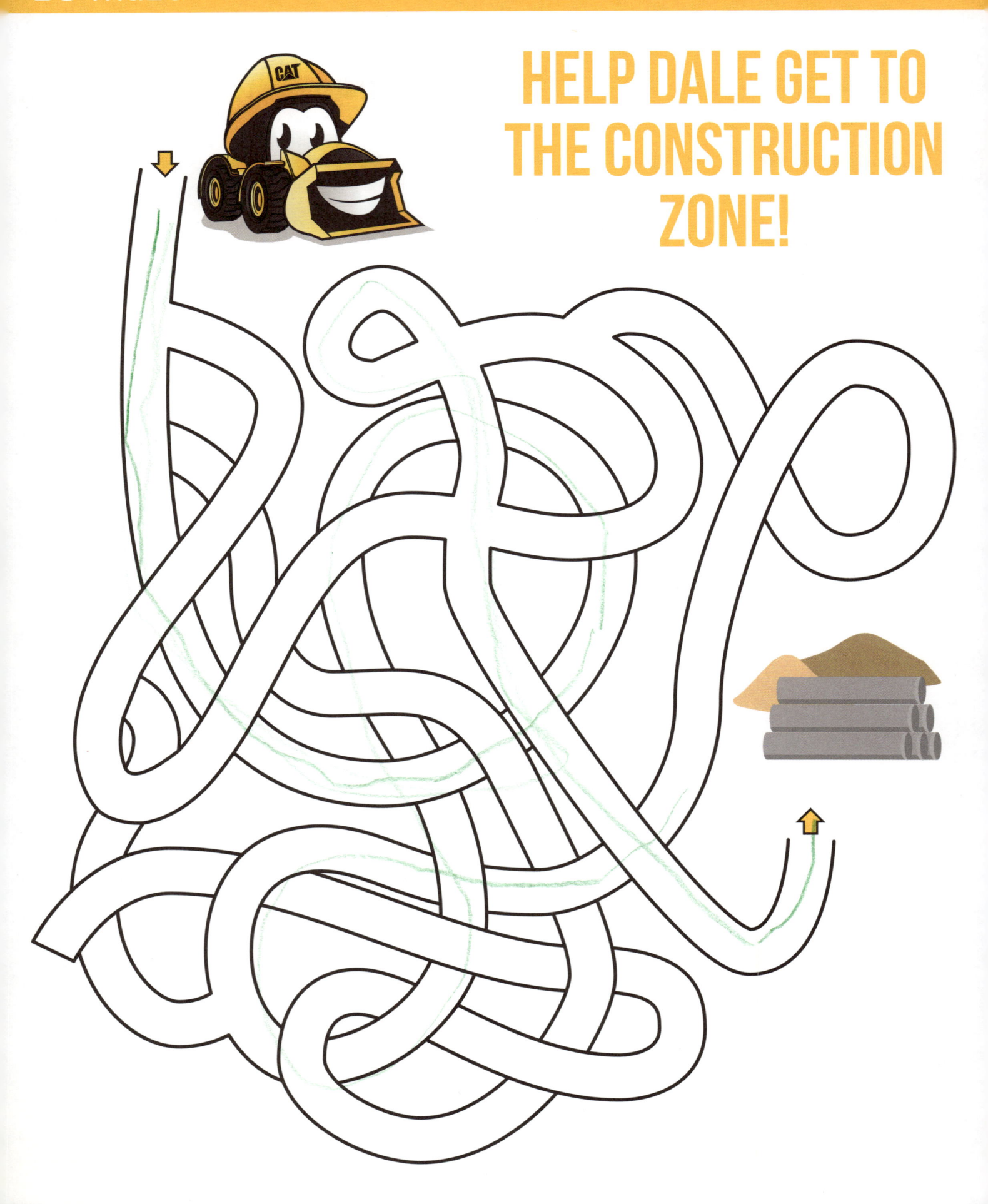

HELP DALE GET TO THE CONSTRUCTION ZONE!

Counting 21

Look at the picture below. Count how many of each objects you see. Write the number on the line next to the object.

22 Shapes

CAN YOU USE THESE SHAPES TO DRAW YOUR FAVORITE CAT® EQUIPMENT?

- CIRCLE
- SQUARE
- TRIANGLE
- RECTANGLE
- RHOMBUS
- HEART

Maze 23

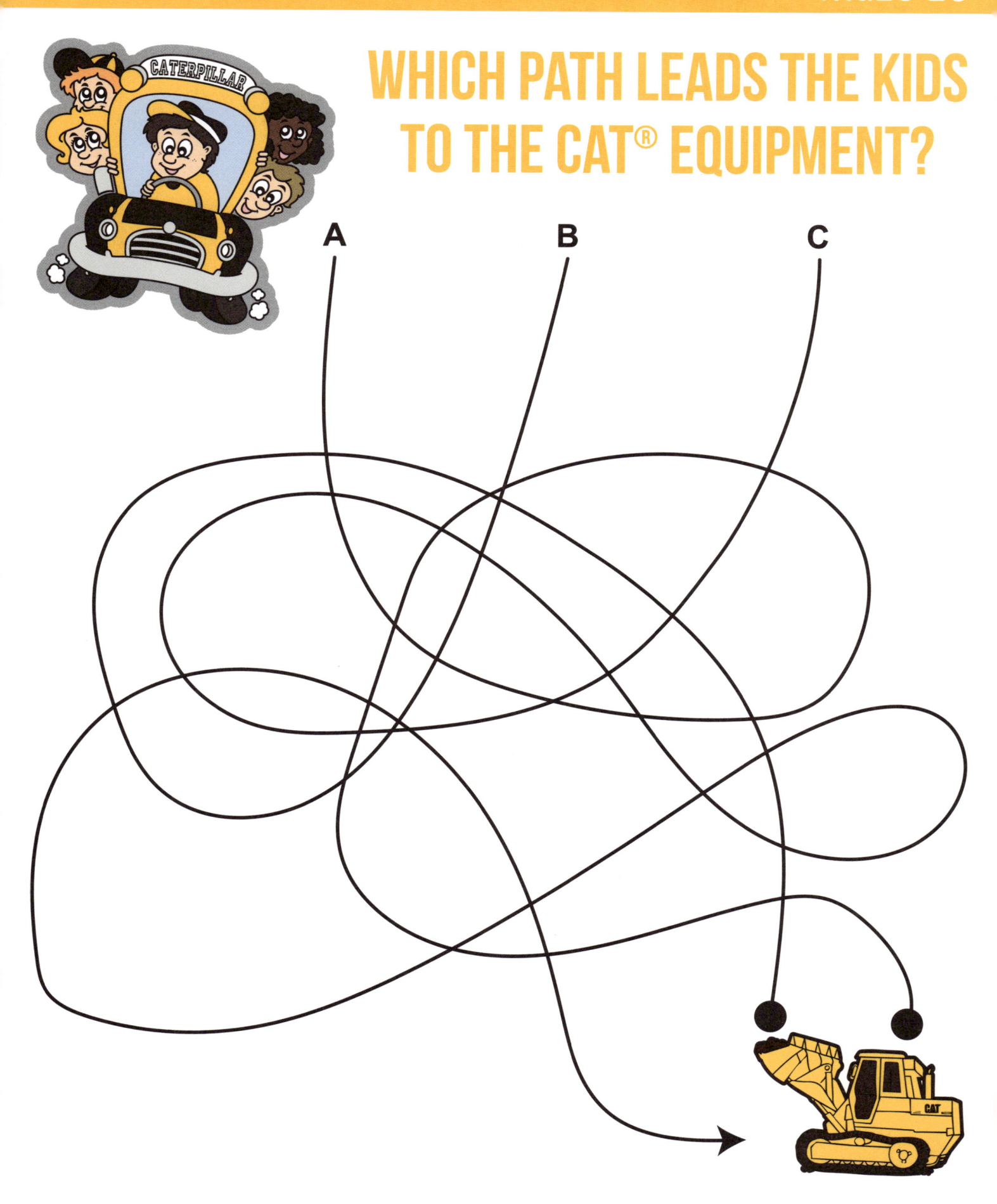

WHICH PATH LEADS THE KIDS TO THE CAT® EQUIPMENT?

A B C

24 Coloring

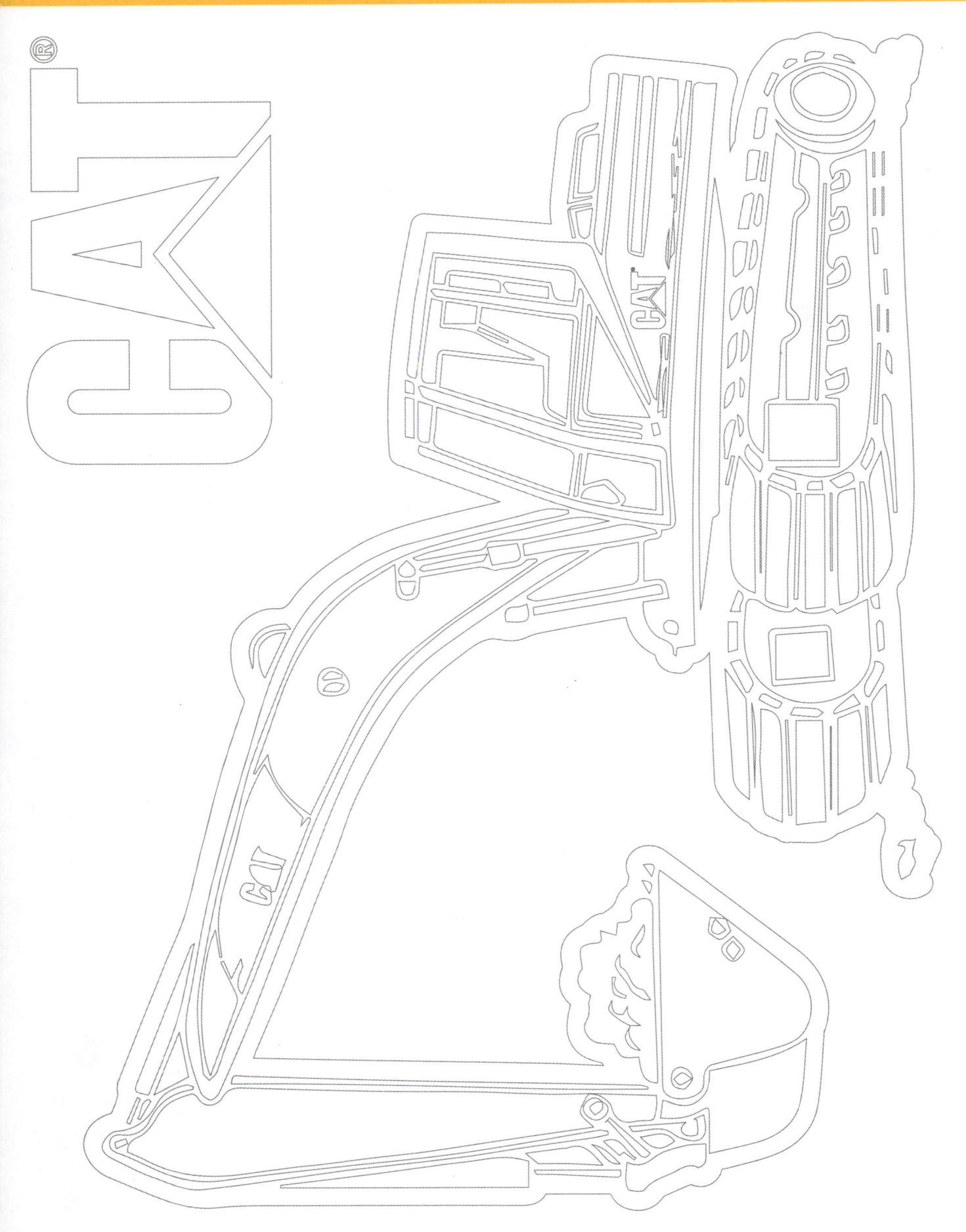

Coloring 25

26 Tic-Tac-Toe

TIC-TAC-TOE

Image Puzzle 27

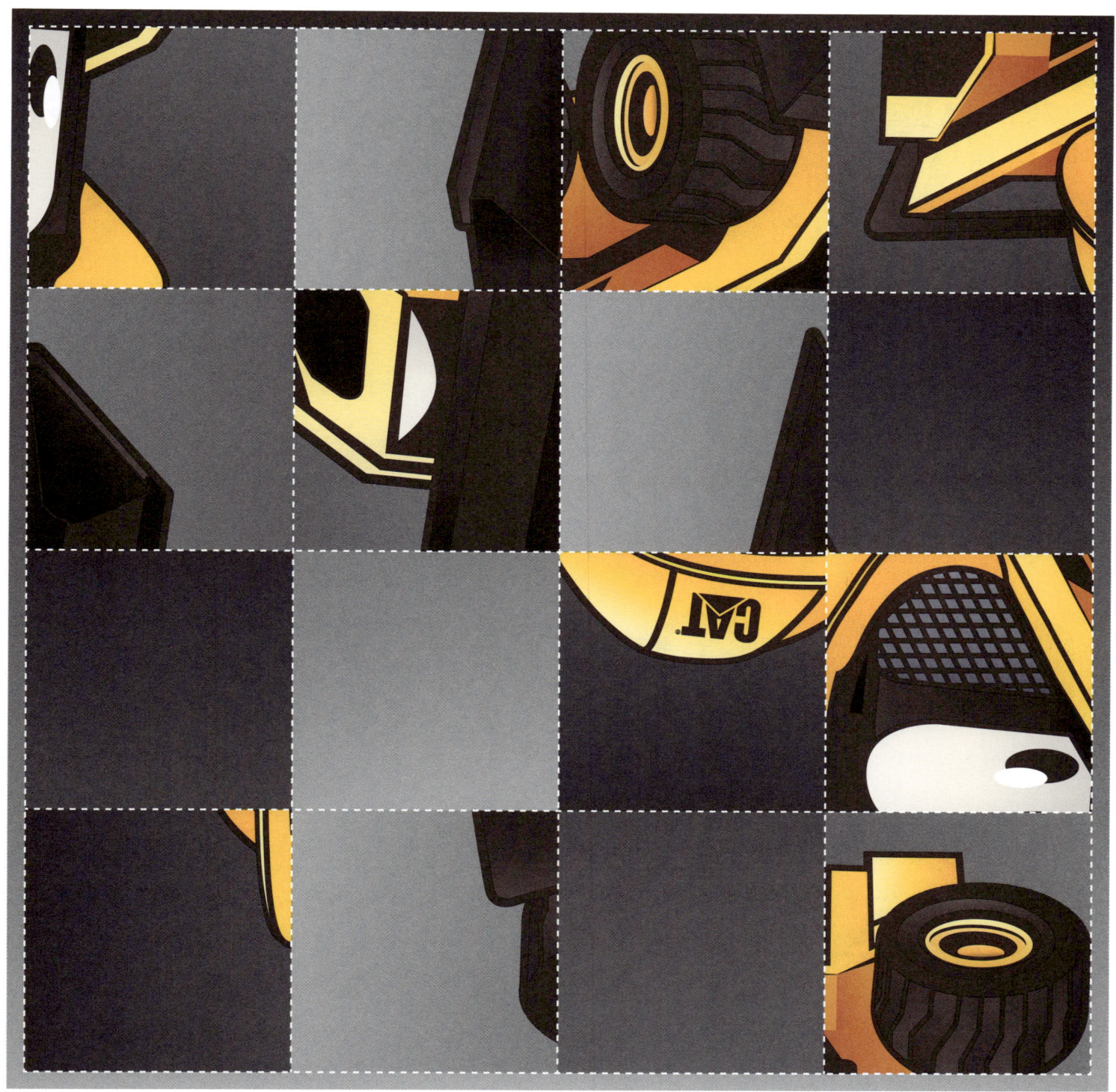

CUT OUT THE SQUARES AND PUT SCOOTER BACK TOGETHER!

28 Logo Cutouts

Digging Time 29

DIGGING TIME!

WHAT TIME DOES THE JOB SITE OPEN?

30 Pix Puzzles

CAN YOU FIND 4 DIFFERENCES IN THESE PICTURES?

Drawing 31

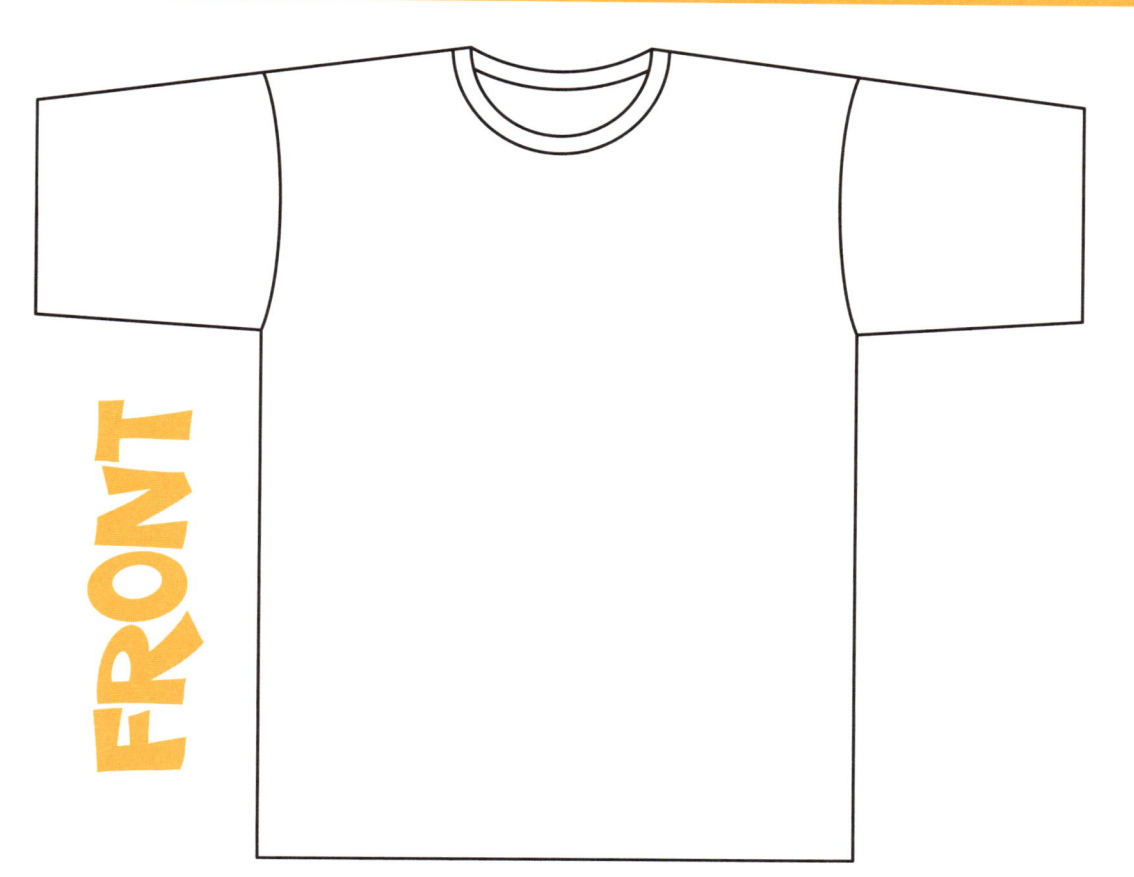

FRONT

DESIGN YOUR OWN SHIRT

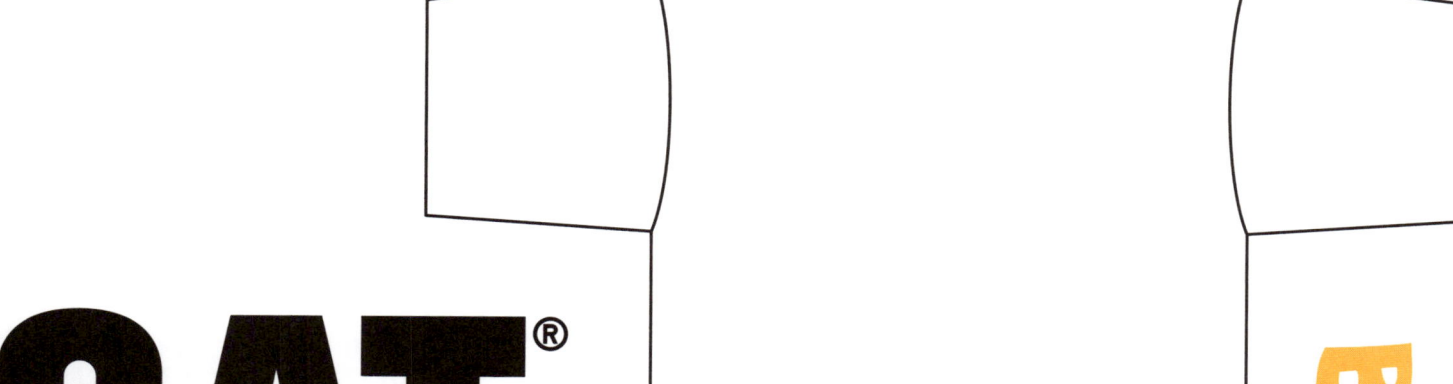

CAT®

BACK

C IS FOR CAT® EQUIPMENT. COLOR THE CIRCLES WITH "C".

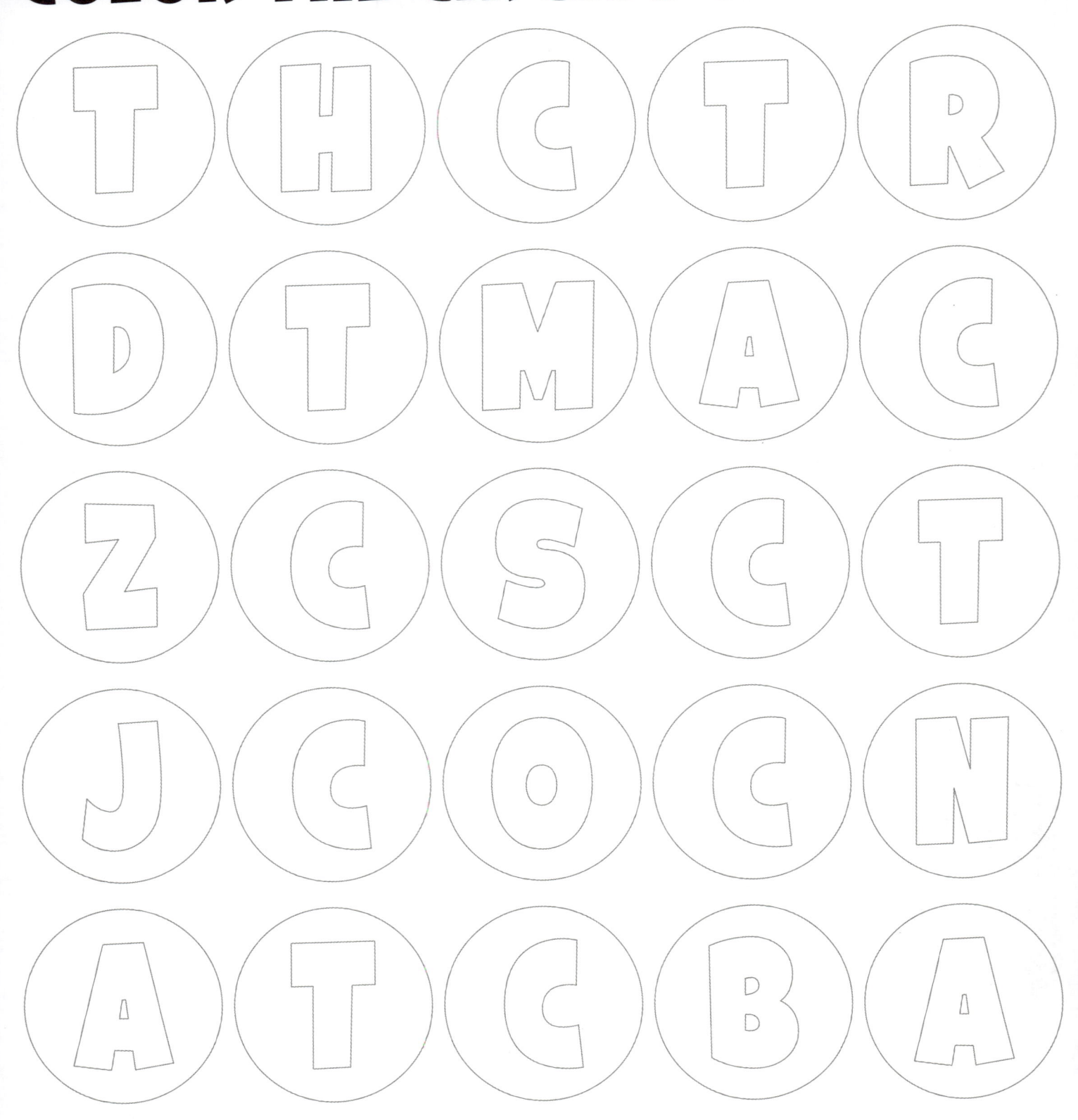

T H C T R
D T M A C
Z C S C T
J C O C N
A T C B A

Games 33

TAKING TURNS, CONNECT A LINE FROM ONE DOT TO ANOTHER. WHOEVER MAKES THE LINE THAT COMPLETES A BOX PUTS THEIR INITIALS INSIDE THAT SQUARE. THE PERSON WITH THE MOST SQUARES AT THE END OF THE GAME WINS!

34 Coloring

Colors 35

RED	+	YELLOW	=	ORANGE
BLUE	+	YELLOW	=	GREEN
RED	+	BLUE	=	PURPLE
RED	+	YELLOW	=	ORANGE
BLUE	+	YELLOW	=	GREEN
RED	+	BLUE	=	PURPLE

36 Coloring

Word Scrambler 37

CAN YOU UNSCRAMBLE THE NAME OF THIS MACHINE?

FRTON EVOSLH

_____ _____

Answer: Front Shovel

38 Writing

THESE WORDS ARE POWERFUL. TELL US WHAT THESE WORDS MEAN TO YOU. HOW HAVE YOU PUT THEM INTO PRACTICE?

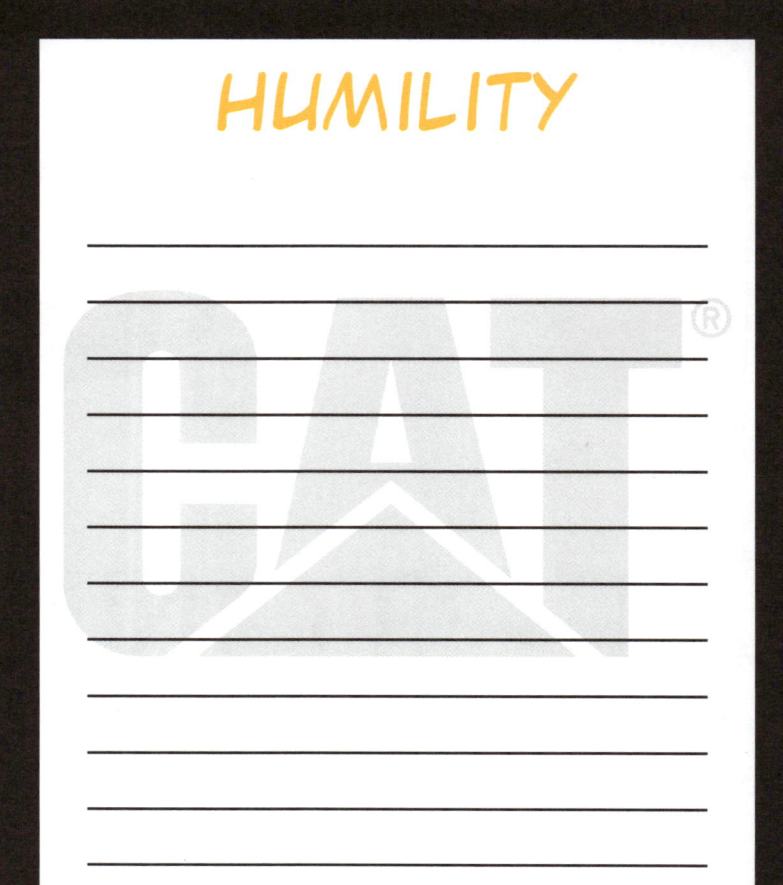

INCLUSION

COURAGE

HUMILITY

Writing 39

RESPONSIBILITY

HEALTH & WELLNESS

RESPECT

PURPOSE

40 Word Search

```
K N O K P S K N Y S Q S S V S
D M Z C I F R A R C T R R E E
S R D Z P A R O P M P E E H N
G H Z Q E S T G T A N L D I I
B P K H L C Y P V A C D A C L
F O R W A R D E R S V N O L G
T S P P Y R R B S L S A L E A
R B M Y E S V O Q R N H C S R
U O Q I R T V E O S H E T X D
C Q J K S C P T S N A L L I E
K O O C Z Z C L E T O E T O J
S R E M I A L C E R E T G Q D
M G A Y R S K I D D E R S Q L
S P Q T S H O V E L S R S Q Z
J F S R E N A L P S R E Z O D
```

CAN YOU FIND THESE WORDS?

COMPACTORS • DOZERS • DRAGLINES
EXCAVATORS • FORWARDERS • HARVESTERS
LOADERS • PAVERS • PIPELAYERS
PLANERS • RECLAIMERS • SHOVELS
SKIDDERS • TELEHANDLERS • TRACTORS
TRUCKS • VEHICLES

Coloring 41

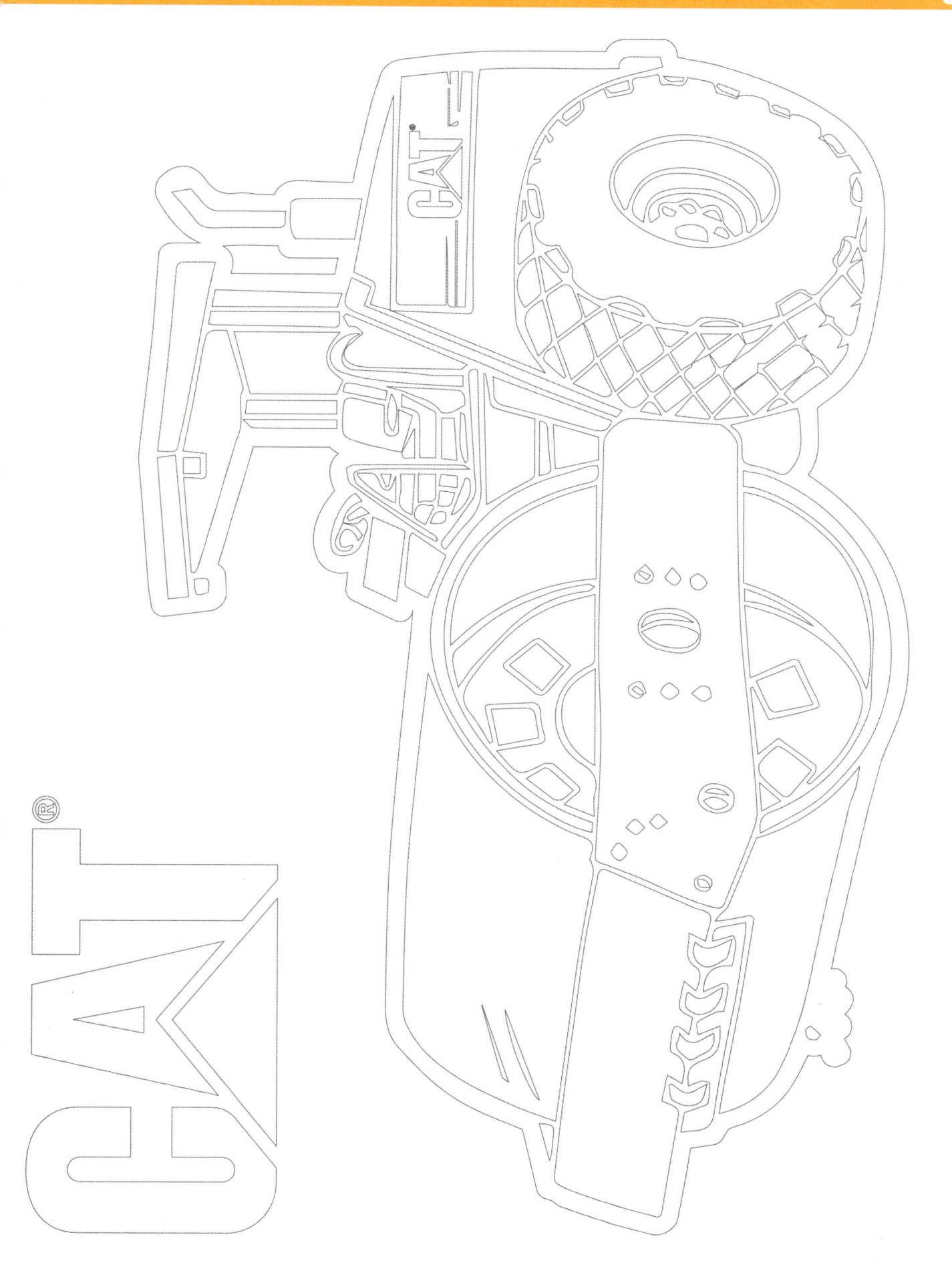

42 Word Maze

USING THE LETTERS IN ORDER TO FORM THE WORD

CATERPILLAR®

FOLLOW THE CORRECT PATH TO FIND YOUR WAY THROUGH THE MAZE.

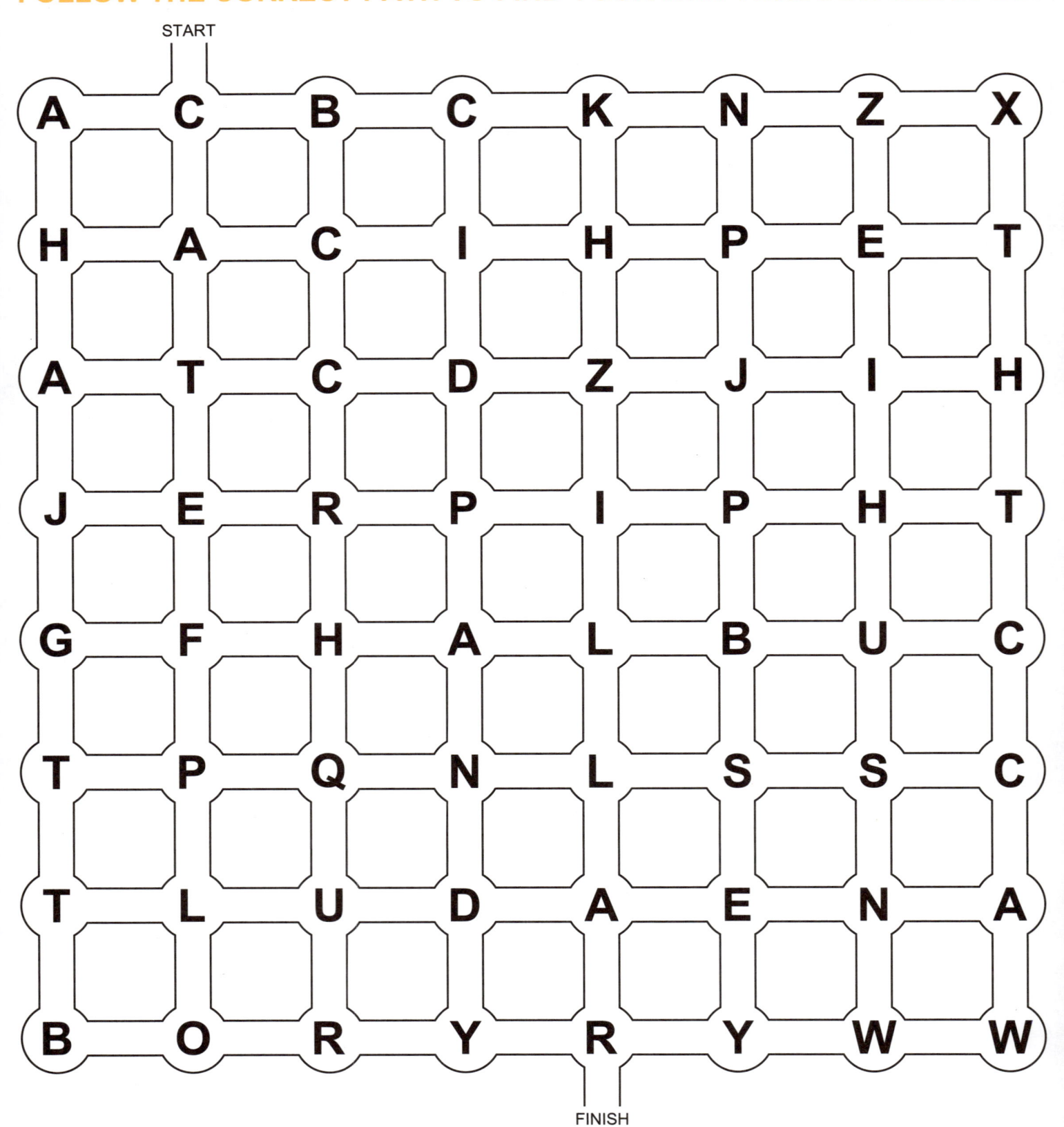

START

A	C	B	C	K	N	Z	X
H	A	C	I	H	P	E	T
A	T	C	D	Z	J	I	H
J	E	R	P	I	P	H	T
G	F	H	A	L	B	U	C
T	P	Q	N	L	S	S	C
T	L	U	D	A	E	N	A
B	O	R	Y	R	Y	W	W

FINISH

Coloring 43

44 Matching

MATCH THE MACHINE TO IT'S NAME

Backhoe Loader

Vibratory Soil Compactor

Track Loader

Soil Compactor

FILL THE RECTANGLE BELOW WITHOUT GOING OVER IT'S EDGES.

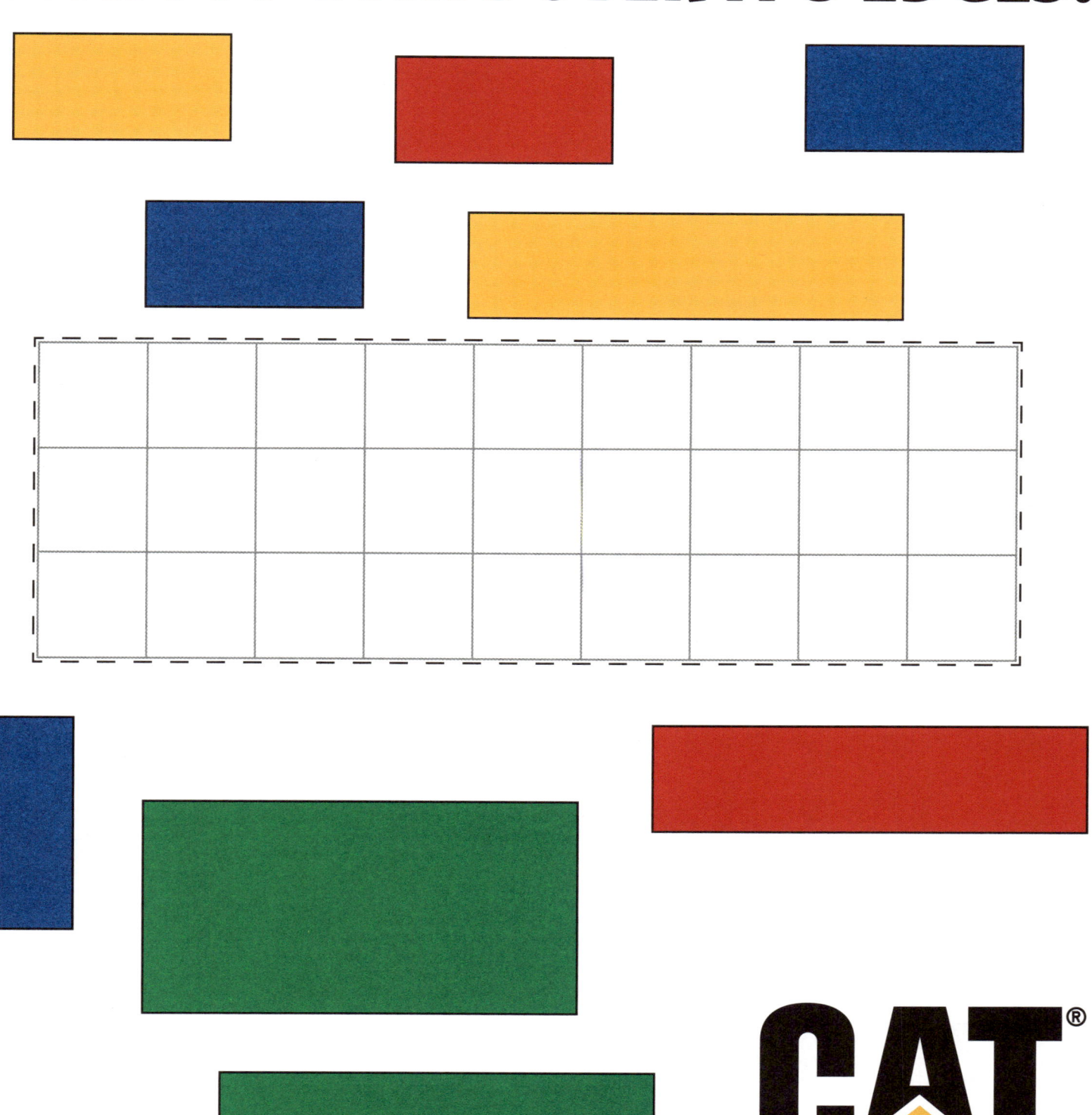

46 Matching

CIRCLE THE CHOMPER THAT IS DIFFERENT.

Coloring 47

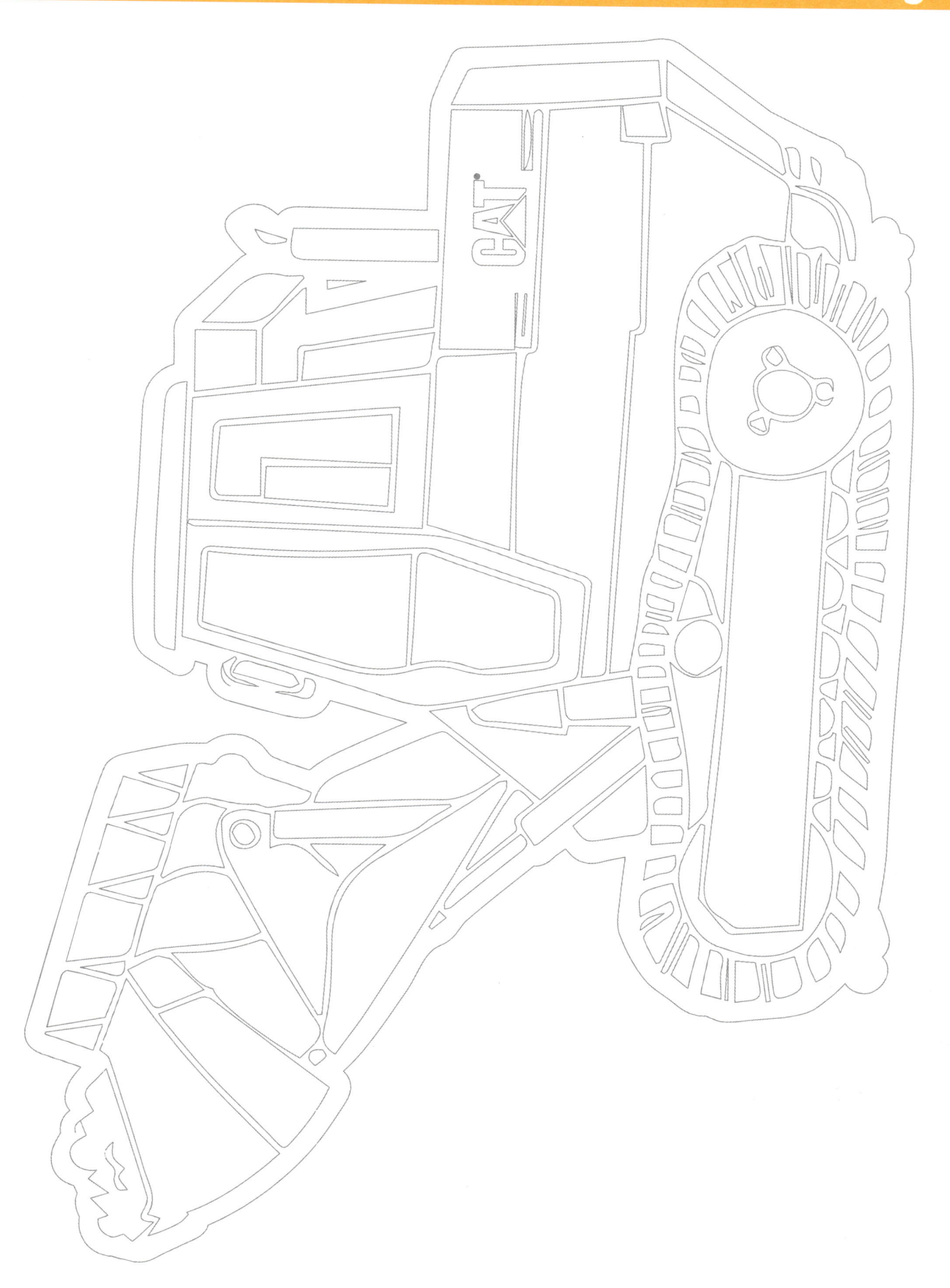

48 Coloring

Darla Hall was born in Indiana and still resides there. She grew up in a small town where she loved playing and watching sports. This book concept was developed in 2012 when a young boy she knew was hit by a car and broke both of his legs. She created her first activity book as a gift for him. Her company, Witty Publications, now has hundreds of titles available at www.wittypubs.com.

Darla Hall

Created by Darla Hall, owner of Witty Publications for the Brush Art Corporation.
www.wittypubs.com | © Witty Publications 2019